Feeling Jealous

For a free color catalog describing Gareth Stevens' list of high-quality books and multimedia programs, call 1-800-542-2595 (USA) or 1-800-461-9120 (Canada). Gareth Stevens Publishing's Fax: (414) 225-0377.
See our catalog, too, on the World Wide Web: http://gsinc.com

The author and original publisher would like to thank the staff and pupils of the following schools for their help in the making of this book: St. Vincent de Paul Roman Catholic School, Westminster; Mayfield Primary School, Cambridge; Swavesey Village College, Cambridge.

Library of Congress Cataloging-in-Publication Data

Althea.
    Feeling jealous / by Althea Braithwaite; photographs by Charlie Best; illustrations by Conny Jude.
       p. cm. — (Exploring emotions)
    Includes bibliographical references and index.
    Summary: Explores the nature of jealousy, how it differs from envy, where these feelings come from, and how to recognize and deal with them.
    ISBN 0-8368-2117-3 (lib. bdg.)
    1. Jealousy in children—Juvenile literature. [1. Jealousy. 2. Envy.]
I. Best, Charlie, ill. II. Jude, Conny, ill. III. Title. IV. Series: Althea.
Exploring emotions.
BF723.J4A57   1998
152.4′8—dc21   98-5584

This North American edition first published in 1998 by
Gareth Stevens Publishing
1555 North RiverCenter Drive, Suite 201
Milwaukee, Wisconsin 53212 USA

This U.S. edition © 1998 by Gareth Stevens, Inc.
First published in 1997 by A & C Black (Publishers) Limited,
35 Bedford Row, London WC1R 4JH. Text © 1997 by Althea Braithwaite.
Photographs © 1997 by Charlie Best. Illustrations © 1997 by Conny Jude.
Additional end matter © 1998 by Gareth Stevens, Inc.

Series consultant: Dr. Dorothy Rowe

Gareth Stevens series editor: Dorothy L. Gibbs
Editorial assistant: Diane Laska

Printed in Mexico

1 2 3 4 5 6 7 8 9 02 01 00 99 98

Feeling Jealous

Althea

Photographs by Charlie Best

Illustrations by Conny Jude

Gareth Stevens Publishing
MILWAUKEE

Jealousy is an awful feeling. We feel jealous when we think someone has something that should be ours. Jealousy can make us very unhappy, and we often will behave badly.

"I used to feel jealous because I thought Mom and Dad gave my brothers all the attention. They never seemed to listen to what I had to say."

Most people feel jealous at one time or another. Can you think of a time when you felt jealous?

Sometimes we feel envious of each other, too.
Envy is wanting something that belongs
to someone else.

*I was envious of
Rob because he was good
at soccer. But I was happy
for him, too, for being
on the team.*

You can be happy for someone at
the same time you're envious.

5

How do you feel when you are jealous or envious of someone?

I want to do something that will really hurt them.

It makes me burst into tears.

Sam remembers, "When my sister was getting ready to go on vacation, I was very nasty to her. After she had gone, I wished I would have said, 'Have a nice time.'"

When my brother was very ill, Mom and Dad spent all their time with him. I felt jealous. I knew I shouldn't, so, at the same time, I felt ashamed.

When you feel jealous, you're the one who is hurt the most. Don't let your feelings take over your life and spoil it.

It's difficult not to feel jealous at times.

When Susie's mom married David, Susie felt jealous because her mom seemed to give David all her time.

"Mom didn't seem to notice me anymore. I didn't like David because I thought he was taking Mom away from me. Now I've come to like him, and they both give me their time."

Becoming a new family takes time. You're likely to feel jealous when other family members seem to be getting all the attention. It's difficult for everyone at first, but it usually all works out.

When their mother picks up Lara and Rob from school, they both want to tell her things. They both feel hurt if they don't get her full attention, and they become jealous of each other.

"I can't split myself down the middle. I try to listen to both of them."

Someone can love more than one person, and love them equally. This love might not appear to be equal, because people don't always show their affection for everyone they love in exactly the same way.

We often envy people who have things we want to have ourselves.

I envy my friend because he's going to Florida this summer. We never go on vacation.

My friend gets twice as much spending money as I do. I can't help feeling a little envious.

"My friend has a huge swimming pool. I love going there. Sure, I envy him, but it doesn't make me angry. I dream about what it would be like to have a pool myself."

Life is not fair, but complaining that it isn't probably will just make you miserable. Envy is normal, but you shouldn't let envy turn into dislike or anger. You'll feel better when you can be happy for a friend who has something special that you don't have yourself.

It's difficult for parents when their children want something new because their friends have it. Parents often don't have the money to buy it, or they refuse to buy it because they don't believe their children should have everything they want.

Mike says, "I envy my friend because she has a computer that does spell check and everything. It's unfair because the computer helps her get better grades on her schoolwork."

Sometimes, after you get what you want, you decide it's not that important to you after all.

"I wanted a radio-controlled car really badly, because my friend has one. When I finally got one for Christmas, I didn't like it that much, but I couldn't tell my parents I didn't."

We sometimes envy people for being able to do something better than we can.

Lara says she envies Susie because Susie is so good at acting.

"At school, she always gets picked for the best parts. I keep practicing at home, so, maybe, I'll get picked for a good part next time."

It's not always a bad thing to envy someone.
It might make you want to try harder to succeed.

Some people find it difficult to share their friends.
They feel jealous when a friend spends time with someone else.

I was very jealous when Jan made friends with Sue. I thought she didn't like me anymore.

When you see a friend with someone else, it doesn't mean he or she doesn't like you. That friend might stop liking you, however, if you behave badly out of jealousy.

At times, even close friends might envy each other.

"When we were younger, Susie came up behind me and cut off some of my hair. Now we are best friends. Her hair has grown longer; mine is cut short."

Brothers and sisters often go through periods feeling jealous of each other. Mike says that, when he was younger, he was jealous of his older brother. "He did everything better than me. Now I get along well with him, but my younger brother is jealous of me."

My sister has a bigger bedroom than mine, and she's younger than me!

Parents usually try to be fair, but they don't always realize how important some things seem to their children. It might help if you try to explain why you mind so much.

Sarah's Room

KEEP OUT!

It can be very annoying when people copy you all the time, but try not to be angry. They copy you because they feel jealous and wish they could be more like you.

When I was younger, I wanted to be just like my sister. I always copied her.

Sometimes, you don't realize that someone is being mean to you because he or she envies you.

"Jim does really nasty things to me. I couldn't understand why he was being so mean. I thought there was something wrong with me. Then my friend told me it's because Jim thinks I'm smart."

Sarah says, "My cousin was always putting me down for being interested in sports. Then I found out he envied me because I'm good at soccer."

When you get angry with someone, it might be because you feel jealous or envious of them. Often it's difficult to admit these feelings, even to yourself.

When someone envies you, you might feel good about it, but be careful not to take advantage of the situation.

"My friend was envious of my new bike. It has lots more gears than his. I kept showing them off to him, and, eventually, he got very angry. Now he's not my friend anymore. I feel bad about that, because he was a lot of fun."

Lara says, "I felt sorry for my friend because she was envious of my running shoes. I told her she was lucky because she had roller skates, and I didn't."

"Shona was envious because I have a sewing machine. I was afraid she might break it, but I told her she could try it out as long as I was there to help her."

If someone envies you, it's all right to try to make them less envious.

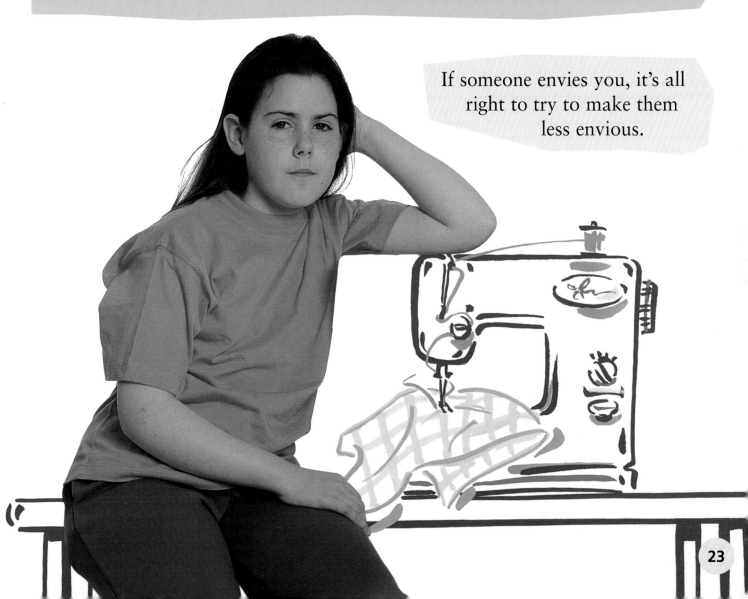

Sometimes you feel envious because you think someone has more than you do. If you get to know all the facts, you might feel differently.

Sam says, "I envied my stepsister because her dad buys her expensive presents. Now I know she hardly ever sees him. I'm luckier, really — I have time with my mom and dad."

Feeling jealous or envious sometimes is natural, but don't let it spoil your life. The best way to handle your feelings is to talk about them. You might be surprised at what you find out!

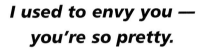

I used to envy you — you're so pretty.

I never knew that! I always envied you because you had so many friends.

For Teachers and Parents
A Note from Dorothy Rowe

Most people feel jealous or envious at one time or another. We feel these emotions when our sense of self-worth is threatened by someone who possesses something we believe is rightfully ours or we want to have ourselves. Jealousy and envy can be accompanied by other emotions, too, such as fear, malice, and even hatred.

Teachers and parents know that children need help dealing with these complicated feelings. Adults sometimes forget, however, that, in order to help, they must be nonjudgmental and must want to understand the child's point of view. A child won't see a situation the same way an adult does for the simple reason that no two people, whatever their ages, ever see things in exactly the same way.

Adults must be prepared to share with children their own experiences, including their struggles with jealousy and envy, and they should not pretend to provide easy solutions.

Children have a strong sense of fairness. They believe that the world is governed by some kind of natural justice. Because of this belief, they also have a keen sense of injustice to themselves when they are being treated unfairly.

Many people have difficulty accepting the possibility that we live in a world where things, good and bad, often happen for no particular reason or through no fault of our own. Those who can't understand and accept this premise can make themselves miserable by feeling cheated and by insisting that the world should be what they want it to be. Life is not fair, but it's much better to make the most of it, rather than dwell on what you think you are missing.

Suggestions for Discussion

Jealousy and envy can be very destructive emotions. Not too many people want to admit, even to themselves, that they feel jealous or envious. Talking about these feelings and realizing that other people have them, too, can help us come to terms with them.

Many of the reasons for jealousy and envy and the ways to cope with these feelings can be discussed with children while going through this book, page by page. The following points might help start your discussions.

Page 4
People feel jealous when they think someone's love or friendship has been taken away from them by someone else.

Page 5
People feel envious when someone else has a possession or an ability they would like to have.

Pages 6-7
Feelings of jealousy and envy can cause strong emotions, which make talking about them difficult. Describing the feeling as a color might make it easier. Jealousy is often called a "green-eyed monster," and people also talk about being "green with envy."

Page 8
Giving love to another person doesn't mean taking it away from someone else. If anything, the more we share our love, the greater our capacity for love seems to grow.

Page 9
People, particularly in families, can appear to favor one person more than another, and, sometimes, they actually do.

Page 12
People who depend on computers to correct their spelling might not learn to spell correctly themselves.

Page 13
You might envy someone because he or she has "the latest" something or other. In a few months' time, however, things probably will change, and something else will be more fashionable or important.

Pages 14-15
Being envious of someone's ability can actually be a good thing if we use our envy to encourage, rather than discourage, ourselves to work hard and improve. If we can admire, instead of resent, the people whose abilities we envy, we might also learn from them.

Page 16
When we lose a friend to someone else, it's easy to blame either that friend or the other person, rather than examine our own behavior.

Page 18
Feeling jealous of brothers and sisters is very common. It often starts when a new baby arrives. Hopefully, being jealous of family members is something people outgrow as they get older.

Page 20
A child who is being teased or bullied by someone who envies him or her often doesn't realize that he or she is the object of envy. A child who lacks self-confidence might even have difficulty believing that anyone would envy him or her.

Page 21
Discovering that someone envies you because you're good at something can be encouraging, particularly if you don't think you're very good.

Page 22
It's not wrong to be proud of something special you have, or to want other people to know about it. "Showing off," however, can easily become annoying, or even hurtful, to others.

Page 23
There are many things you can do to try to reduce the jealousy or envy someone else feels about you or something you have. At times, however, nothing you do will help.

Page 25
Allowing feelings of jealousy or envy to overwhelm you can be very destructive. You might come to believe that you are not as valuable or as fortunate as other people, and you could end up losing your self-confidence.

More Books to Read

Being Me. Life Education (series).
    Alex Parsons (Watts)

Emotional Ups and Downs.
    Good Health Guides (series).
    Enid Fisher (Gareth Stevens)

If You Had to Choose, What Would
    You Do? Sandra M. Humphrey
    (Prometheus Books)

What Would You Do?
    A Kid's Guide to Tricky and
    Sticky Situations. Linda Schwartz
    (Learning Works)

Why Do Kids Need Feelings?
    A Guide to Healthy Emotions.
    Monte Elchoness (Monroe Press)

Videos to Watch

Hey! That's Not Fair.
    (Film Ideas Inc.)

I Hate My Brother Harry.
    (Churchill Media)

Jealousy Is No Fun. Our Friends on
    Wooster Square (series).
    (Franciscan Communications)

No Fair! (Sunburst Communications)

Web Sites to Visit

www.pbs.org/adventures/   KidsHealth.org/kid/feeling/

Due to the dynamic nature of the Internet, some web sites stay current longer than others. To find additional web sites, use a reliable search engine with one or more of the following keywords to help you locate information about jealousy and envy. Keywords: *behavior, conflict, emotions, envy, feelings, friendship, green-eyed monster, jealousy, resentment, rivalry.*

Glossary

admit — to tell the truth about something; to confess.

affection — a feeling of warmth for someone; fondness for or a caring attachment to another person.

ashamed — feeling guilty and sorry for something you did that you know is wrong.

attention — the act of focusing your thoughts and activities on the needs and wants of someone or something that interests you.

behave — to act in a particular way that is considered correct or proper.

complain — to express discomfort, unhappiness, or disappointment, often in an irritating way.

copy — to act or look, as nearly as possible, like someone or something else; to imitate.

envious — wanting something that someone else has, sometimes to the point of disliking or being nasty to that person.

jealous — feeling hostile toward someone who has things or advantages that you think should be yours.

miserable — extremely uncomfortable or unhappy.

moody — feeling and acting gloomy, unhappy, or unfriendly.

nasty — very unpleasant, short-tempered, and mean.

selfish — thinking only of yourself; putting what you want ahead of what others need.

take advantage — to use another person's kindness or weakness in a mean or selfish way to get something you want.

understand — to recognize, accept, and care about the circumstances of another person.

Index